When Children Pray

Samantha Pegues

Published by: Pegues Enterprises

ISBN: 9780692470909

Dedication

This book is dedicated to my nephews, Justin, Dre, JaRecus (RIP), Tay, CJ, Jahmal, Bricen, and Cooper; my niece, Tia; my great-nieces Adaysia, Kailyn, Christian, and Ivory; my godchildren Xavian, Samuel, Ty, and Kennedi; and to all of the children in the world. You are special to God.

Contents

Following the Rules

On the first day of school, CJ and Cooper walked into their classroom. Mrs. Dalton had written on the board an important rule for her class: *Keep your hands, feet, and all other objects to yourself!*

Cooper asked, "Why do we have to follow that rule?"

CJ replied, "It is important to follow the rules given by teachers and our parents. Rules help to keep us and those around us safe. We must remember that no one should ever put their hands on us or hit us with any objects while we are at school. If someone touches us, we must quickly tell an adult. Although rules may seem silly or hard to follow, we must obey them to avoid getting hurt or hurting someone else."

CJ began to pray: Dear God, you are our protector. There is safety in you. Thank you for keeping us safe even when we don't obey the rules of our parents and teachers. Forgive us for not following your instructions. Help us to keep your commandments and follow the rules given to us by adults. Teach us how to be respectful and obedient children. Amen.

When children pray, following the rules becomes easier.

God's rule: "Children obey your parents in the Lord, for this is right"
- Ephesians 6:1, ESV

What other rules do your teachers and parents have for your safety?

My child, pay attention to what your father and mother tell you.
—Proverbs 1:8, GNT

Differences

Sherron and Shannon are twins. Although they look alike, they are very different. Sherron's favorite color is yellow, but Shannon loves purple. Sherron's best friend is a boy named Carlos. Carlos is not from the United States. He is from South America, and he can speak Spanish. He says, "¿Que pasa?" instead of saying, "What's up?" Shannon's best friend's name is Charles. Sherron and Shannon have been having a hard time at school. The other students tease them because of their best friends' race. Shannon and Sherron are black, but Carlos is Hispanic, and Charles is white. The white girls and boys say mean things to them like, "You need to stick with your own race," while the black ones say, "How can you be friends with someone whose ancestors made your ancestors slaves?" It hurts their feelings when the other children make those comments because they weren't raised to judge people by the color of their skin. Their parents taught them to love people for who they are on the inside, not by how they look on the outside. When Sherron looks at Carlos, she sees someone who makes her laugh when she's sad. When Shannon looks at Charles, she sees a boy who always gives her treats and walks her home from school to make sure that she's safe.

It is important to remember to treat all people with respect. God created us in different colors, shapes, and sizes, but we're all equal even though we might not look the same or speak the same language. However, God loves us all the same. Did you know that we are all God's children? Even adults! God loves all of the children in the world. He loves them regardless of their race. So should you!

Sherron began to pray: Dear God, you are so creative! Thank you for making us all different because life would be so boring if everyone was the same. If we all looked and sounded alike, you might get our prayers mixed up. But, because I am unique and there is no one in the whole world like me, I know that you hear me every time that I pray and you know exactly where to find me. God, forgive us for judging people by their race. Teach us how to love and get along with everyone. Help us to understand that we are all brothers and sisters because you are our Father. Change our hearts so that we will treat each other like family regardless of the color of our skin. Amen.

When children pray, they are able love with a pure heart.

What God says about racism: "If we say we love God, but hate others, we are liars. For we cannot love God, whom we have not seen, if we do not love others whom we have seen" – 1 John 4:20, NLT

Love your neighbor as yourself.
-Matthew 22:39, NIV

Keep on loving each other as brothers and sisters.
-Hebrews 13:1, NIV

Bullying

Lori was taller than everyone in her class. The other children called her names like "giraffe" and "Big Bird." This caused Lori to feel very hurt and depressed. Therefore, she started bullying the other children to make herself feel better. She took their lunch money and made them carry her books to class. She also threatened to beat them up if they talked about her.

One day, Lori began to tease a girl named Jessica who was much smaller than her. She pulled Jessica's hair and pushed her around every time that she saw her. Jessica became very afraid of Lori because she was twice her size, and even if she tried to defend herself, she probably wouldn't win. So Jessica told her teacher about all of the mean things that Lori had done to her. However, Mrs. Slate replied, "Jessica, stop tattling and learn how to stand up for yourself!" That made Jessica feel even more afraid and helpless because not only was Lori bullying her at school, she was also spreading a lot of rumors about Jessica on the internet. As a result, Jessica became too depressed and ashamed to go to school. She often pretended to be sick so that she could skip school. Jessica's mom noticed her sudden change of behavior, and she questioned her. Jessica told her mom that she was being bullied, and she no longer wanted to go to school. She also said that she wished that she was never born. Jessica's mom immediately called the principal, and Lori was expelled from school.

Bullies come in all shapes, sizes, and colors. You may be bullied for being black, white, a boy, a girl, or for being rich or poor. Did you know that some students are even bullied for making good grades? Can you believe that? Remember that it's not your fault that you're bullied. Bullies aren't happy with themselves. Therefore, they try to make themselves feel better by making others unhappy. It's important to have courage when you're faced by bullies. You should never allow them to see you cry or show any signs of being afraid because bullies live off of fear. Being bullied can make you feel lonely, angry, and depressed. However, quitting school or committing suicide is never an option to avoiding bullies. Always walk with a group of friends and tell more than one adult that you're being bullied.

Jessica began to pray: Dear God, you are so brave. Thank you for keeping me safe from bullies. Make me deaf to the mean things that bullies say. Give me wisdom to ask the right person for help. Help me to understand that asking for help is a sign of strength, not weakness. Surround me with friends who have the courage to stand up for me. Please teach bullies how to feel good about themselves so that they won't try to make me feel bad about myself. God, give me the courage to face my enemies and teach me how to love them even when they say mean and hateful things about me. Amen.

When children pray, they find courage to face their fears.

God's defense against bullies: "For God did not give us a Spirit of fear but of power and love and self-control" – 2 Timothy 1:7, NET

Blessed are the peacemakers, for they will be called the children of God.
-Matthew 5:9, NIV

See that no one pays back evil for evil, but always try to do good to each other and all people.
-1 Thessalonians 5:15, NIV

Passing Difficult Tests

Math is the hardest subject for most students because it forces them to develop and use critical thinking skills. Our math teacher, Mr. Buford, always tells us, "If there is something that you don't understand, or if there's something that you are having problems with, come talk to me before or after class and I will help you. Do not wait until test day to ask me a question because I will not talk to you after I pass out the tests."

Nick and Audrey were both failing their math class, but they were too ashamed to ask for help. They did not want the other children to make fun of them. Thankfully, they saw Mr. Buford in the hallway, and they asked him for help.

Did you know that God is the best teacher? Every day, he gives us a chance to ask him for what we need and for help with the things that we don't understand through prayer. Like Mr. Buford, sometimes God is also silent when we are going through tests. During these times, God wants us to develop and use critical praying skills. He has given us the Bible as a study guide so that we're prepared for life's most difficult tests. The good thing about it is that all of our tests are open-book tests, and we can open the Bible to find all of the answers.

Nick began to pray: Good morning, God! You are an awesome teacher! Thank you for teaching us the things that we don't understand. Forgive us for not asking for your help first. Help us to realize that there is no failure in you, and that asking for help doesn't mean that we're dumb. It's actually a sign that we're growing and learning. Give us the ability to easily remember what we have studied and read. God, give us the faith, wisdom, and knowledge to graduate to the next level in you and in school. Amen.

When children pray, they are able to pass their most difficult tests.

God's answer key: "For I can do all things through Christ who gives me strength" – Philippians 4:13, NLT

If you do not have wisdom, ask God for it. He is always ready to give it to you and will never say you are wrong for asking.
-James 1:5, NLV

Don't ever forget God's formula for your life:
GOD > my problems= Truth

Forgiveness

One day, while playing around outside, Ty accidently pushed Kennedi down. Kennedi began to cry because she scraped her knee. Ty immediately apologized to Kennedi, and she forgave him. However, Kennedi's older brother, Samuel, heard about what happened. He wanted to fight Ty because he loved his little sister more than anything. Kennedi explained to Samuel that it was an accident and that Ty had already apologized, and she had forgiven him. However, Samuel still could not forgive Ty. So, Kennedi asked her brother, "Do you remember when you accidentally pushed me down? I forgave you, so why can't you forgive Ty?" Samuel then realized that he couldn't forgive Ty because he hadn't forgiven himself for accidentally hurting his sister.

Sometimes it's hard to forgive others who have hurt us or someone we love. However, it's very important to practice forgiveness, because holding on to grudges may cause us to become angry and violent. It may also cause us to have health problems. More importantly, grudges are held in our hearts. Therefore, unforgiveness destroys our hearts. Did you know that unforgiveness can block our prayers from being heard by God? We should never give anyone that much power over us. We must ask God for forgiveness and ask him to help us to forgive ourselves and others on a daily basis so that he will hear and answer our prayers.

Samuel began to pray: Father God, you are so nice. You are a forgiving God. Thank you for forgiving us even when we don't forgive others. God, create in us a clean heart so that we might forgive others and be pleasing in your sight. Help us to understand that we don't have the right to hold grudges against anyone because you never held one against us. Give us the courage to say, "I'm sorry" when we do others wrong and teach us how to let go of the things that we can't change. Amen.

When children pray, they are able to find forgiveness in their hearts.

God says: “If you forgive others the wrong they have done to you, your father in heaven will also forgive you” – Matthew 6:14, NIV

Can think of a time when you wanted someone to forgive you? What happened?

Holding on to a grudge hurts you more than the person who you hold it against. Let it go!

Safety

Casey grew up on a farm where there were many chickens. One day, Casey heard his chickens making a lot of noise. So, he ran outside to see what was going on. He saw a hawk flying toward his chickens, and the mother hen was signaling for her baby chicks to come to her. The mother hen spread her wings as her chicks ran toward her. After all of them were safely under her wings, she closed her them so that the hawk couldn't harm her baby chicks. As a result, the hawk flew past them because it was afraid of the mother hen and they were all safe.

The next day at school, Casey was talking to his friends, Camille and Brandi, at lunch when all of a sudden they heard what sounded like gun shots. Casey remembered that just as his chicks ran to their mother for safety, he could also run to God in the time of danger. He immediately grabbed his friends by their hands, and they ran behind one of the pillars across the room. As a result, they were safe from danger.

Casey began to pray: Dear God, you are absolutely amazing! You are our sword and shield. Thank you for your protection. Please forgive us for kicking you out of our schools. God, we ask you to please come back because we realize that we need you here to protect us from guns and all other forms of violence. God, please keep us safe in our homes, at school, sporting events, church, and everywhere we may go. Lord, be our personal bodyguard from all hurt, harm, and danger. Please make our school a pray-ground. Amen.

When children pray, they find safety.

God's safety tip: "The name of the Lord is a strong tower. The righteous run to it and are safe" – Proverbs 18:40, NLT

Read Psalm 91 every day before leaving and entering your house. It is a psalm of protection.

You should never take any weapons to school. If you see someone with a weapon, immediately tell an adult.

When Someone Dies

Sasha's mother has a heart disease. When people have a heart disease, their heart and blood vessels don't work the way that they should, and it makes them very sick. Sasha's mother has been in the hospital for three months. Although she goes to visit her mom every day after school, Sasha still seems a little sad. I try to cheer her up by doing things that make her laugh. It works for a little while, but then I notice that she's sad again.

Today, I went with Sasha to visit her mom. Her mom wasn't feeling so well, and she was having problems breathing. The doctor told us that we had to leave the room. So Sasha kissed her mom and told her that she loved her. We waited in the hallway for a long time. Finally, the doctor came out and told Sasha and her dad some very sad news. Sasha's mom had passed away. Sasha began to cry. Her dad gave her a big hug and told her that everything was going be alright.

No one lives forever; therefore, it's important that we live each day as if it is our last. We should tell our friends and family that we love them as much as possible. It's also important to eat a healthy diet and exercise regularly so that we may live longer lives.

Sasha began to pray: Dear God, you are the giver of life. Thank you for giving me my mother. I wish that she could have stayed with me a little while longer, but I know that you know what's best for her even though I might not understand why she had to leave me. Give me strength and peace during the times when I miss her most. You said in your word that when my mother and father leave me, you will take care of me. God, I ask you to comfort me during this time of sadness. Thank you. Amen.

When children pray, they are able to find peace during difficult times.

God says: "He will wipe every tear from their eyes, and there will be no more death or sorrow or crying or pain. All these things are gone forever" (Revelation 21:4, NLT).

If we live, we live to the Lord; and if we die, we die to the Lord. So, whether we live or die, we belong to the Lord.
-Romans 14:8, NIV

Dear friend, I pray that you may enjoy good health and that all may go well with you...
-3 John 1:2, NIV

When I Grow Up

Today was career day at school. Angel and Grace came dressed as nurses. When Mrs. Martin asked them why they wanted to become nurses, they told her that they wanted to save people's lives. Katie was dressed as a police officer because she wants to protect good people from bad guys when she grows up. Chad came dressed as a football player because he wants to play professional football. Brice came dressed as a preacher because he wants to pastor a church someday. Mrs. Martin praised them for having such awesome goals. However, she explained to them that they must learn to develop honesty and integrity in order to become successful in their careers.

Did you know that God also has plans for your life? It is important ask God what are his plans for your life. It is also very important to have dreams and goals. Without them, you will lose focus and the desire to do well in school. You may want to become a pastor, a doctor, a teacher, or you may want to play professional sports. However, you must first desire to be a person of good character.

Brice began to pray: Dear God, you are the perfect role model! Thank you for your plans for our lives. Forgive us for making plans without you. God, we ask you to show us the plans that you have for us and lead us into that direction. Teach us how to be children of integrity so that we will not have any children without being married first and so that we will never spend a night in jail when we grow up. We will grow up to be world changers who live out the promises of God. Amen.

When children pray, they develop integrity and wisdom to make their dreams come true.

God's plan: "For I know the plans I have for you, says the Lord. They are plans for good and not disaster, to give you a future and a hope" – Jeremiah 29:11, NLT

The righteous man walks in integrity; His children are blessed after him.
-Proverbs 20:7, NKJV

What do you want to be when you grow up? Why?

Family

Most of the children at school think that Tay and Tia have a perfect family. Their dad, Charles, is a lawyer, and their mom, Mary, is a doctor. Tay and Tia wear the best clothes and shoes, and their parents buy them just about every new toy and video game that comes out. Tay and Tia pretend as if they have a picture-perfect life at school. However, at home, it is a totally different story. The truth is that they only see their father twice a week and they only see their mother three times in a week because of their work schedule. Their mother is always too tired to help them with their homework, and their dad never has time to attend their soccer games on Saturdays. Both parents yell at them if they ask for help with their homework because they're so tired and stressed out from work. On top of that, Tay is always playing his video games, and Tia talks on her cell phone until bedtime every night. Therefore, they don't have a close relationship.

While Tay and Tia love all of the nice things that their parents buy for them, they love their parents even more. They would rather spend more time with their parents than have all of the latest toys and video games. Did you know that God also wants to spend time with you? You can spend time with God by praying, singing to God, or reading the Bible.

Tay began to pray: Dear God, you are the perfect parent! Thank you for always having time for us. Forgive us for not spending enough time with you and our family. Help our parents to understand that while we may need money, we need their time, love, and support just as much. Please don't let our parents be too tired to spend time with us and pray with us. Help them to deal with the stress from their jobs so that they won't yell at us when we accidentally get too loud or ask for their help with our homework. Teach my sister and me how to spend time with each other before we play our video games or talk on the phone. God, please draw us closer together as a family and teach us how to balance our daily lives. Amen.

When children pray, families grow closer together.

God's advice for families: If a house is divided against itself, that house cannot stand –Mark 3:25, NIV

Fathers, do not aggravate your children, or they will become discouraged.
- Colossians 3:21, NLT

What can you do to spend more time with your family?

I Am Important

Have you ever felt lonely and sad? Or ever felt depressed because you didn't feel like you fit in with the other students? Maybe you felt that way because of the color of your skin. Or maybe you felt like you weren't as pretty or as handsome as some of your classmates. You might have even felt as if you didn't belong because you just weren't an important person. Well, that's not true! You are important and very special to God! Let me show you.

There was a shepherd, named Howard, who had one hundred sheep. He knew them all by their names. One day, he took them out to the pasture to eat. After they were done, he led them back toward his house. About halfway home, Howard decided to stop and count his sheep to make sure that they were all with him. He realized that he was missing one of his sheep. The sheep's name was Linda. This caused Howard to become tearful because he loved all of his sheep, and he couldn't imagine living without one of them. So, he left the ninety-nine sheep and ran back to find the one that he was missing. When he saw her, his face lit up with joy. He screamed, "Linda! There you are my precious child!" Howard was so excited that he ran and hugged Linda. He even picked her up and carried her back home instead of allowing her to walk because he did not want her to get lost again.

Did you know that God is our shepherd? He knows us all by our names. You don't ever have to feel lost, lonely, or depressed when you don't fit in because God knows exactly where you are, and he will always come to your rescue. Even when you think that you're alone, God is always with you. Not fitting in with a crowd is not always a bad thing. Sometimes, it just means that you're special and unique! Some people are born to standout!

Pray with me: Dear God, you are the coolest God! Thank you for making me feel better when I am lonely and depressed. Forgive me for not liking myself and for complaining about the way that I look.

Help me to not feel sad when I am not accepted by others. Teach me how to be confident in you and how to be happy with myself. Help me to understand that I am not going to always fit in with the crowd. That doesn't mean that I'm not good enough or cool enough to hang out with them. It just means that their group is not for me. God, thank you for allowing me into your circle of friends. You love and accept me just the way that I am, and for that you will always be my number one friend. Amen.

When children pray, they begin to realize how special they are.

What does God say about children? "Children are a gift from the Lord; they are a reward from him" – Psalm 127:3, NLT

Let the children come to me. Do not stop them! For the Kingdom of God belongs to those who are like these children. -Luke 18:16, NLT

Unless you change and become like little children, you will never enter the kingdom of heaven. -Matthew 18:3, NIV

Anger

Hi, my name is Sonya. Sometimes I feel angry when things don't go my way. I don't know why I feel this way. I just do. When my mom tells me to clean my room, sometimes I do it. But, sometimes I don't feel like it, and I get mad when she keeps telling me to. I wish that she would just give me a break! I mean, after all, it's my room, and I'm the only one who has to sleep in here! I remember when I punched a hole in the wall because I was so angry. Not only am I angry at home, but I have also gotten angry at school. Sometimes, it's hard for me to sit still and concentrate while the teacher is teaching, and I often get in trouble for talking and acting out. The school counselor told my mom and me that the doctor may have to put me on medication to make me calmer if I don't learn to control myself. I don't want to take any medicine! I mean, it's not like I'm crazy! I just can't seem to control myself sometimes. I don't like being like this, but I just don't know what to do.

Sonya began to pray: Dear God, you are a patient God. Thank you for not staying angry with me when I mess up. Forgive me for letting my anger get out of hand. Teach me how to control my temper and help me to become a better child and student. I understand that it's natural to get mad sometimes but teach me how to talk about what's bothering me instead of acting out. Surround me with people who will be patient with me and pray with me. God, I really want to be a better person. Please help me to be a calm and obedient child and replace my anger with patience and love. Amen.

When children pray, they learn to control their temper.

God says: "Everyone should be quick to listen, slow to speak and slow to become angry, because human anger does not produce the righteousness that God desires" – James 1:19-20, NIV

And don't sin by letting your anger control you...
-Ephesians 4:26, NLT

A hot-tempered person starts fights; a cool-tempered person stops them.
-Proverbs 15:18, NLT

Single Parents

Dre lives with his mother, Roberta, and his sister, Brittany. Their mother has been struggling to pay their bills for the past two months because their father moved to another state after their divorce. Not only has Roberta been struggling, Dre and Brittany have been having a hard time as well. Dre has become very angry since his father left, and Brittany has become depressed because she misses her father. Dre has been getting into trouble a lot at home and at school while Brittany seems to be sad all of the time. She stays in her room and doesn't talk to her family and friends anymore.

There's another child, named Tanner, who used to live with his mom and dad until the police came and took his dad away for committing a crime. Tanner's mom has also been struggling to pay their bills because she is the only one in the house who has a job. Before Tanner's dad left, they all followed a chore chart. It was Tanner's responsibility to clean his room and take out the trash. It was his mom's job to wash the dishes, and his dad was in charge of cutting the grass. But now that Tanner's dad is gone, he also has to do his dad's chores. Tanner tries to cut the grass, but he can't cut it like his father used to. This is very stressful for Tanner because not only does he have more chores to do, he also has to babysit his three younger sisters while his mom goes to work. On top of that, he also feels ashamed when the other children tease him because his dad is in jail.

It is hard when parents get divorced. However, it is important to remember that it is not your fault. Sometimes adults just don't get along well. We must also remember not to make fun of people who have a parent who is in jail. If you have a parent who's in jail, you don't have to be ashamed. No one is perfect. Everyone makes mistakes—even adults!

Dre began to pray: Dear God, you are the world's greatest father! Thank you for your love and support. Forgive us for trying to do everything on our own. God, my mother can't teach us everything. There are some things that only a father can teach us. Surround us with godly men to show me how to treat females and to show my sister how males should treat her. Help us to understand that our parents' divorce is not our fault. Give my mother wisdom to make more money so that we won't worry about what we're going to eat, what we will wear, or where we're going to live. Teach us how to be respectful to our dad even when he's not around. Please help my parents to make the right decisions so that we can stay together as a family. I'm only a child, and there's no way that I can take my dad's role in our home. God, please

be the man of our house. Amen.

When children pray together, families grow closer together.

God's says: "God in His holy house is a father to those who have no father…" –Psalm 68:5, NLV

Honor your father and your mother, so that you may live long in the land the Lord your God is giving you.
-Exodus 20:12, NIV

Fathers, do not provoke your children to anger by the way you treat them.
-Ephesians 6:4, NLT

Sharing

Courtney and Daisy are next-door neighbors. Daisy's family had to move in with Courtney's family because their house was torn down by a tornado. Sometimes Courtney tended to be mean to Daisy because she didn't want to share a room with her. Courtney would often say, "I'll be glad when you go back to your own house," and "Your mom needs to buy you your own stuff." This made Daisy feel very sad because she thought that Courtney was her friend. However, what hurt her most was the fact that Courtney told everyone at school that Daisy was living with her family because she had nowhere to live. Well, Daisy's house was finally finished a few weeks later and she moved back home. She continued to friendly with Courtney even though she had said some very hurtful things. Unexpectedly, a few months later, Courtney's mom and dad lost their jobs because the company that they worked for shut down. Therefore, Courtney's family had to move in with Daisy's family because her mom and dad could no longer afford their house. But, unlike Courtney, Daisy happily shared her room and belongings with Courtney, neither did she tell anyone at school that Courtney's family had to move in with her family.

It's important to share with other people because we never know when we will need someone to share what they have with us. We should never make anyone feel bad for needing our help, and we should never gossip about their situation with other people. How would you feel if someone told all of your secrets? Remember that the most important thing that we could ever share is our love.

Daisy began to pray: Dear God, you are our shelter. Thank you for sharing your love with us. Forgive us for being selfish and for gossiping about people. Teach us how to share with a good attitude and without expecting anything in return. Help us to realize that we all need each other's help. Create in us a clean heart so that we will be kind and merciful to others. Help us to understand that you have blessed us to be a blessing to others. God, you shared your only Son with the world.

The least we can do is share the things that you have given us to help others. Please give us a pure heart and helping hands. Amen.

When children pray, they are able to share with a loving heart.

God says: "And do not forget to do good and to share with those in need. These are the sacrifices that please God" – Hebrews 13:16, NLT

For God loved the world so much that he gave his one and only Son, so that everyone who believes in him will not perish but have eternal life.
-John 3:16, NLT

It's always better to share love than hatred.

Friendships

Justin and Kevin are best friends. They live in the same neighborhood, they go to the same school, and they attend the same church. Justin and Kevin have been friends since they were three years old. One day, a new boy, named Kareem, moved into their neighborhood. Kareem had been kicked out of his first school for bad behavior. Therefore, his family moved to Kevin and Justin's neighborhood so that he would be able to go to school.

Around the third week of school, Kevin started hanging out with Kareem. Justin chose not to hang out with them because he didn't like the things that they were doing. Kareem began to tease the other children, and he also stole their belongings.

Because of this, Justin said to Kevin, "Man, I don't think that you should be hanging out with Kareem. He's going to get you in a lot of trouble."

Kevin replied, "So what? Do you think that you're better than us?"

Justin answered, "No. I don't think that I'm better than you. I love you like a brother, and I just don't want to see you get into any trouble."

"Man, whatever," Kevin replied as he angrily walked away.

Later on that day while everyone was at lunch, Kareem asked Kevin to go back to the classroom with him to get his cell phone. Kevin agreed. Kareem went into another student's backpack and stole his cell phone. Kevin didn't know that the phone didn't belong to Kareem. As they were walking out of the classroom, Coach Babb saw that Kareem had a cell phone in his hand, and he took it away from him. Coach Babb discovered that the phone belonged to his son, Matt. As a result, Kareem was suspended from school for stealing. Even though Kevin had no idea that the phone was stolen, he was also suspended because he was with Kareem when it was stolen.

Justin began to pray: Dear God, you are my best friend. Thank you for encouraging me to do what's right. Forgive me for following the bad advice of the people who I hang around. Teach me how to stand up for what is right without being afraid of how my friends will react. Surround me with friends who bring out the best in me. Help those who I choose not to hang around understand that I don't think that I'm better than them. I have just chosen to follow a different path. Teach me how to not be judgmental and gossip about the things that they choose to do. Instead, help me to pray that they change their ways. God, teach me how to be a true friend who loves at all times. Amen.

When children pray, they choose their friends more wisely.

God says: Do not be deceived: "Bad company ruins good morals" – 1

Corinthians 15:33, ESV

A friend loves at all times.
-Proverbs 17:17, NKJV

Even small children are known by their actions…
-Proverbs 20:11, NIV

Leadership

A leader is a person who guides a group of people or country. Leaders can be found just about anywhere in the world. Parents are leaders of their homes. Teachers are leaders of their classrooms, while the principal is the leader of the whole school. Pastors are the leaders of churches, and the president leads our country.

One night, Destiny was watching television with her mom, Shirley, and she saw some very sad news. Millions of people were homeless and did not have a job because of a worldwide war. On top of that, millions were also in hospitals and many lost their lives because of the war. Destiny began to cry because she felt so sorry for all of the people who were hurt.

She asked her mom, "Why do we have to have wars and kill innocent people? Can't we all just get along? I wish that there was something that I could do to help those hurting people."

Shirley replied, "We go to war because our leaders won't agree to make the best decisions for everyone in a peaceful manner. While we can't control the actions of our leaders, we can always pray for them."

Destiny began to pray: Dear God, you are the best leader ever! Thank you for showing us the right path. Forgive us for not always following your instructions. God, please help our parents, bus drivers, teachers, policemen, and pastors to become the best leaders that they can be. Please protect all of our leaders; including our president. Keep him and his family safe from all danger. Help him to make the best decisions for our country. Give him the courage to stand up for what's right and not what's popular. Don't allow him to make decisions out of greed or selfishness. Encourage him to fight for our freedom of religion and freedom of speech. Give him clean hands and a pure heart. Touch the hearts of all of the leaders of the world and help them to understand that it's better to live in peace than it is to go to war. Amen.

When children pray, nations are changed!

What does God say about leadership? “When the righteous are in authority, the people rejoice; But when a wicked man rules, the people groan” – Proverbs 29:2, NKJV

What are some characteristics of a good leader?

The Lord is my shepherd; I shall not want.
-Psalm 23:1, KJV

Children are the greatest people in the world! Don't believe me? Check this out!

God says: "Whoever becomes like this little child is the greatest in the kingdom of heaven" – Matthew 18:4, GWT

When children pray, they realize that they are filled with greatness!

www.ingramcontent.com/pod-product-compliance
Ingram Content Group UK Ltd.
Pitfield, Milton Keynes, MK11 3LW, UK
UKHW021834270726
14058UKWH00001B/152